The Bear
and the

The Characters

 Narrator

 Bear

 First Bee

 Second Bee

 Third Bee

 Narrator: One day, Bear saw a big beehive. The bees did not like the bear.

 First Bee: Buzz buzz. Get away from here. Do not take our honey.

 Bear: Grrr grrr! I like honey. The honey is mine.

 First Bee: It is not!
The honey is ours.
We made it.
Go away or you
will be sorry.

 Narrator: But Bear did
not go away.

 Second Bee: Buzz buzz.
Get away from here.
Do not take
our honey.

 Bear: Grrr grrr!
I like honey.
The honey is mine.

 Second Bee: It is not!
The honey is ours.
We made it.
Go away or you
will be sorry.

 Narrator: But Bear did not go away.

 Third Bee: Buzz buzz. Get away from here. Do not take our honey.

 Bear: Grrr grrr! I like honey. The honey is mine.

8

9

 Third Bee: It is not!
It is ours. We made
it. Go away or
you will be sorry.

 Narrator: But Bear
did not go away.
He looked in the hive.

 Bear: Grrr grrr!
I like honey.
I will eat the honey.
The honey is mine.

 Third Bee: The honey is ours. Go away or you will be sorry.

 Bear: I will not go away.
I will eat the honey.
The honey is mine, mine, mine.

 Narrator: Then all the bees buzzed from the hive. They buzzed and buzzed and buzzed.

 Bees: Buzz buzz buzz.
Get away
 from our honey.
Take that and that
 and that.

Narrator: The bees chased Bear away. All Bear got for his mine, mine, mine was lots of stings.